The History of Basing House, in Hampshire ...
Tenth edition. [With an engraving of Basing House.]

Anonymous

The History of Basing House, in Hampshire ... Tenth edition. [With an engraving of Basing House.]
Anonymous
British Library, Historical Print Editions
British Library
1858
50 p. ; 8°.
10362.g.59.

The BiblioLife Network

GUIDE TO FOLD-OUTS, MAPS and OVERSIZED IMAGES

THE
HISTORY
OF
BASING HOUSE,

IN HAMPSHIRE,

CONTAINING AN INTERESTING ACCOUNT OF THE SIEGE
IT SUSTAINED DURING THE CIVIL WAR;

WITH

NOTICES OF CELEBRATED PERSONS

CONCERNED IN ITS TRANSACTIONS;

With an Appendix,

Containing (Peter Lockhart's) Letter to the Speaker of the House
of Commons, on the Storming of Basing House, &c.;

AND

TWO LETTERS TO THE MARQUIS OF WINCHESTER,
TO SUMMON HIM TO SURRENDER.

TENTH EDITION.

CHARLES EDWARD HUNTER.—HORACE.

BASINGSTOKE:

PRINTED AND SOLD BY SAMUEL CHANDLER.

1869.

J. M. Stroud
Sulhamstead

THE

HISTORY

OF

BASING HOUSE,

IN HAMPSHIRE,

CONTAINING AN INTERESTING ACCOUNT OP THE SIEGE
IT SUSTAINED DURING THE CIVIL WAR;

WITH

NOTICES OF CELEBRATED PERSONS

CONCERNED IN ITS TRANSACTIONS;

With an Appendix,

Containing Oliver Cromwell's Letter to the Speaker of the House
of Commons, on the Storming of Basing House, &c.;

AND

TWO REPLIES TO THE MARQUIS OF WINCHESTER,
TO SUMMONSES TO SURRENDER.

———

TENTH EDITION.

———

Spectandus in certamine Martio,
Devota morti pectora liberæ
QUANTIS fatigaret RUINIS.—HORACE.

———

BASINGSTOKE:
PRINTED AND SOLD BY SAMUEL CHANDLER.
1858.

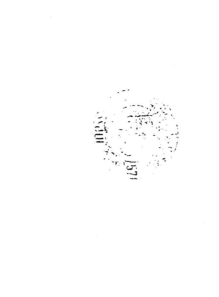

J. Busen. sculp.

ADVERTISEMENT.

The siege of BASING HOUSE constitutes one of the most eventful pieces of history during the civil war, in the reign of Charles the First, when JOHN PAWLET, Marquis of Winchester, made it a garrison for the king, which he defended with prodigious courage and resolution for two years. This stately palace was at length taken and destroyed by Cromwell, and the action is numbered among his greatest exploits. The present publication, for the compilation of which the publisher is indebted to a literary friend, may perhaps be found interesting to many readers, as containing a variety of information collected from various sources. It is hoped, that it may be particularly acceptable to those who reside in the vicinity of OLD BASING, who may have visited the ruins, which still exhibit the remains of ancient strength and splendour, or may have heard of the arduous and tedious siege which it sustained in the civil wars of the seventeenth century.

ADVERTISEMENT TO TENTH EDITION.

In presenting a Tenth edition of the History of the siege of Basing House to the public, the publisher can but thank his friends for the eagerness with which they have purchased the former impressions. Had the literary friend who furnished him with materials for this history been alive, and in the neighbourhood, this edition would, in all probability, have contained an additional number of interesting circumstances; as it is, the publisher has done his best, and given, in the shape of an appendix, much information respecting the final assault and capture of the noble mansion, together with the plunder it contained. These particulars are stated in Oliver Cromwell's letter to the speaker of the House of Commons—account of col. Hammond, delivered at the bar of the House—and the relation of Hugh Peters to the same body. We scarcely need add, that these documents are authentic, and must be highly interesting to the lovers of ancient remains in our own neighbourhood.

THE
HISTORY
OF
BASING HOUSE.

BASING, or OLD BASING, is a considerable
village in Hampshire, about two miles north-east
from Basingstoke. The name is Saxon, and signi-
fies a coat of mail, to which it is said to bear some
resemblance,* referring, perhaps, to its military
strength. That it was, previous to the conquest, a
place of more importance than Basingstoke, there
is no reason to doubt, from the Saxon addition of
Stoke, (or hamlet) added to the latter. Basing is
also memorable for a bloody battle fought between
the Danes and the Saxons, commanded by king
Ethelred and his brother Alfred, in the year 871, in
which the latter were defeated. It became still more
famous, however, for the gallant stand made against
the forces of the Parliament, in the reign of Charles

---

* Bailey's Dict.

the First, by John Pawlet, Marquis of Winchester, a lineal descendant of Hugh de Port, who, at the period of the Domesday survey, held fifty-five lordships in this county. Basing, the head of these extensive possessions, appears to have been very early the site of a castle, as mention of the land of the old castle of Basing, occurs in a grant made by John de Port, to the neighbouring priory of Monk's Sherborne, in the reign of Henry the Second.* William, his grandson, assumed the name of St. John; and Robert, lord St. John, in the forty-third of Henry III., obtained a licence to fix a pole upon the bann of his moat at Basing, and also permission to continue it so fortified during the king's pleasure.† In the time of Richard II., Basing, with the other estates of the family, was transferred, by marriage, to the Poynings; and again, in the time of Henry VI., to the Pawlets, by the marriage of Constance, heiress of the former, with Sir John Pawlet, of Nunny Castle, Somersetshire.

Sir William Pawlet, third in descent from this couple, created Baron St. John of Basing, by Henry VIII,; and Earl of Wiltshire and Marquis of Winchester, by Edward VI., was a very polite nobleman, and greatly in favour at court, through most

---

* Gentleman's Mag. 1787.   † Ibid.

of the successive changes that occurred in the reigns of Henry VIII., Edward VI., Mary, and Elizabeth. He held the office of treasurer nearly thirty years. Being asked how he contrived to maintain his situation in such perilous times, wherein so many great changes had taken place in church and state, he answered, " by being a willow and not an oak."* He re-built the castle at Basing in a magnificent and even princely style, so much so, indeed, that Camden, in allusion to the vast expense of living entailed on his family by its splendor, observes, that " it was so overpowered by its own weight, that his posterity have been forced to pull down part of it."

Here king Edward VI. was entertained by the Marquis of Winchester, with his retinue, for four days. Philip and Mary, whom the Marquis had accompanied to Winchester, after their marriage, were also entertained here for five days.† Here also, in the year 1590, he entertained Queen Elizabeth with all good cheer, and so much to her satisfaction, that she playfully lamented his great age; " for by my troth," said the delighted sovereign, " if my lord treasurer were but a young man, I could . find in my heart to have him for a husband before any man in England."‡ This nobleman died in

---

* English Peerage·   † Oxford Mag. April, 1770.
‡ Queen Elizabeth's Progresses, Vol. I. p. 56.

1572, at the age of ninety-seven, having lived to
see one hundred and three of his own immediate
descendants; he was buried in Basing church.

William, his great grandson, and fourth Marquis
of Winchester, had likewise, in the year 1601, the
honour of having Queen Elizabeth for a guest, and
that for a period of " thirteen days to the *greate
charge* of the sayde Lorde Marquesse."   During her
residence here, the Duke of Biron accompanied by
about twenty of the French nobility, and a retinue of
about four hundred persons, were lodged in the Vine,
the seat of Lord Sandys, which house had been pur-
posly furnished with hangings and plate from the
tower and Hampton Court, " and with sevenscore
beds and furniture, which the willing and obedient
people of the countrie of Southampton, on two dayes
warning, had brought in thither, to lend the Queene."*
When Elizabeth departed from Basing, she affirmed,
that " she had done that in Hampshire, that none
of her ancestors ever did, neither that any prince
in Christendome could do: that was, she had, in her
progress at her subjects' houses, entertained a royal
ambassador, and had royally entertained him." This
Marquis died in 1628, at Hawkwood, now Hackwood, the present seat of his descendants.‡

---

* Queen Elizabeth's Progresses, Vol. II. p. 5.
† Ibid, Vol. II.   ‡ Beauties of England and Wales, Vol. VI.

John, his son, the fifth Marquis of Winchester, was the brave nobleman who rendered his name illustrious by his gallant defence of BASING HOUSE, in the cause of Charles I, during a tedious siege and blockade, or rather a succession of them, which, with short intermissions, continued upwards of two years.

This noble mansion was built upon a rising ground, and was surrounded by a brick rampart, which was lined with earth, and all encompassed with a dry ditch. Basing House is not to be confounded with the castle, to the east of which it was situated, at a small distance; some remains of the foundations still exist.

In the beginning of the civil war, this garrison much distressed the Parliamentarians by the command it had of the western road, insomuch that it was several times besieged by their forces under Col. Norton, Col. Morley, and Sir William Waller, who greatly distressed, but could not take it. The Marquis declared, that "if the king had no more ground in England than Basing House, he would hold out to the last extremity." At first there were none but the Marquis' own family, and one hundred musqueteers from Oxford, but afterwards the King supplied him as occasion required. To inspire the garrison with courage and perseverance in the resolute contest, he wrote with a diamond in every window

the words, *Aimez Loyaulté*; for which reason the
house was called Loyalty House, and the words in
French, *Aimez Loyaulté*, afterwards become the motto
of the family arms, as they are to the present day.

The investment commenced in August 1643 ; the
first material assaults were made by Sir William
Waller, (called, from his former successes, William
the conqueror) who thrice, within nine days attempted
to take it by storm, with seven thousand men, but
was repulsed, and obliged to retreat, with great loss,
to Farnham.

The following journal of interesting transactions,
relative to the siege, which we now proceed to present to the reader, is extracted from a publication
entitled, " His Majesty's Happy Progress and Success, from the 30th of March to the 23rd of November, 1644." By Sir Edward Walker, Knt , Garter
Principal King at Arms, and Secretary of his Majesty's Council of War.

Aug. 14. " Now, in this time of expectation, we
had leisure to enquire after the actions of those rebels
we had left behind us, and what conditions His Ma-
justy's garrisons stood, whereof BASING we left besieged, and Banbury and Dennington castles, were
since surrounded by the rebels.

Sept. 11. " Having many difficulties to pass before
he made his winter quarters, likewise remembering

that Basing and Banbury were then closely besieged."

Sept. 20. " And now it will be fit to observe the gallant behaviour of his Majesty's garrisons of Banbury, Dennington, and Basing, with what success the rebels had in continuing those sieges.

"The last in order, though first in action, is the garrison of Basing, which had now nearly sixteen weeks defended themselves against the collective body of Norton's, Onslow's, Jarvas's, Whiteheads, Jones', and Morley's forces, all colonels under the rebels; though the chief commander there was Norton. And it was now more than time to think of the relief of that place, which was accordingly the ninth of the present September performed with no less courage, than singular success, by forces drawn out of his Majesty's garrisons of Oxford and Wallingford, under the conduct of that discreet commander Col. Gage. For the manner of this action I shall refer you to this extract relation, penned by himself, and addressed unto Lord Digby, principal Secretary of State, which was received at Chard the 29th following.

My Lord,
            It hath pleased the lords here, having lately commanded me out upon an expedition of his Majesty's service, to command me now to write to your lordship a true relation of that service; in which, as there is nothing meriting your knowledge,

you must expect to have the truths I shall tell but
lamely related by my unskilful pen. In obedience,
therefore, to their lordship's commands, I departed
out of Oxford, upon Monday night, the 9th of this
month, with somewhat more than 400 musqueteers
of his Majesty's and colonel Hawkins' regiment, and
250 horse of my lord treasurer's regiment, commanded by colonel Webb, of Sir Arthur Aston's regiment, commanded by lieutenant colonel Bunkle, and
the horse of Borstail House, commanded by lieutenant colonel Campion, twelve barrels of powder,
1200 weight of match, with order to relieve Basing
House, (long besieged by the rebels) and put in such
provision of victuals as the country there affords.
With these troops I marched towards Wallingford,
where I found captain Walter with about fifty horse
of his troop, and as many foot of that garrison:
and having marched all night, we reposed and refreshed our men upon Tuesday morning, at Chaulsey.
From whence I despatched an express to Sir William
Ogle, governor of Winchester Castle, who had pro-
mised Mr. Secretary Nichols, 100 horse and 300 foot
of that garrison to help to raise the siege of Basing,
whensoever the lords should have any such design.
I sent, by this express, a letter of credit of Mr.
Secretary's to Sir William Ogle, desiring him, with
his men, to fall into Basing park, in the rear of the

rebels' quarters there, betwixt four and five of the
clock in the morning, being Wednesday, the 11th of
September; whilst I, with the troops of Oxford, fell
on upon the other side, and my lord Marquis,
from within the house, plied them with sallies.
Having despatched this express, and refreshed my
men, I marched forward, with as much speed as the
soldiers could march, towards Aldermaston, where I
intended to repose and refresh again, passing through
the country for parliament men, with orange tawny
scarfs and ribbands in our hats. Thither I sent captain Walters before with his troop, and the quarter-
masters of each regiment to have provisions in a
readiness against the soldiers arrived, intending only
to refresh and rest two or three hours. But captain
Walters, finding some parliament scouts in that town,
forgot his orange tawny colours and fell foul with
the enemy, taking six or seven of them prisoners, by
which he unmasked and discovered us to be royalists.
But at last the gross of our troops arrived thither
about eight, and rested till eleven o'clock, upon Tuesday night, and then set forwards again, and marched
all night, arriving within a mile of Basing betwixt
four and five o'clock upon Wednesday morning; our
foot being extremely surbated and weary, though I
had endeavoured to ease them what I could in the
whole journey, either by setting them up behind the

horsemen, or making the horsemen alight and the foot ride, or by encouraging them with hopes of great pillage, or with promises of money when they returned to Oxford. I was no sooner arrived there, but lieutenant Swainely met me, sent by Sir William Ogle, from Winchester, to tell me that he durst not send his troops to assist me, in regard some of the enemy's horse lay betwixt Winchester and Basing; so that I was forced to enter into new councils, and call the officers together to take new resolutions. And because we were disappointed of so considerable a party as that of Winchester, and presuming the enemy might draw to a head, having notice of our coming, we resolved not to dismember our forces, and fall on at several places, (as we would have done if either of the Winchester forces had arrived, or we could have surprised and taken the enemy at unawares) but to fall on jointly at one place. In order to which, I commanded the men to be ranged into battalions, and riding up to every squadron, gave them what goods words and encouragement I was able, (though I confess it needed not, most of them being so well resolved of themselves) and delivered them the word (St. George,) commanding every man to tie a white tape, ribband, or handkerchief, upon their right arm above the elbow, which was the sign and word I had formerly sent to my lord Marquis, (lest by his sallying and our falling on we might, for want of a distinctive sign, fall foul of each other.) We marched on, col. Webb leading the right wing, and lieutenant col. Buncle the left wing, of the horse, and myself the foot, till, at the upper end of a large champian field, upon a little rising or ascent of a hill, near certain hedges lined by the enemy's musqueteers, we discovered a body of five cornets of horse standing in very good order to receive us. But before we could come up to them we were saluted from the hedges with a smart volley of musket shot, more terrible than damageable; for col. Webb, notwithstanding, with the right wing of my lord treasurer's horse, charged the enemy so gallantly, that in a moment they all turned head and ran away; lieutenant col. Buncle with our left wing falling in likewise after them, and following the chase with the right, till the rebels' horse were gotten into a place of safety. In this pursuit, what men or horse of the enemy were lost, I cannot learn certainly; but certain I am, we took a colour or cornet, of their's, which I understand was col. Morly's, the motto of which was *Non ab Equo sed in Æquo Victoria;* a a motto not so proper to theirs, as our cause, the equity of which gave us the victory, with true and genuine signification of the motto. On the routing of their horse, I advanced with our foot, and after

two hours disputing the business, beat them from
hedge to hedge, till at last they abandoned all their
quarters and works on that side, and give me free
entrance into the house: where, after I had put in
the ammunition I had brought with me, and paid
my lord Marquis the respects due to a person of his
merits and quality, and leaving him in the house 100
whitecoats of col. Hawkins' regiment, I marched,
with the rest of the horse and foot, towards Basingstoke, a town a mile distant from Basing House,
and, with a small resistance, possessed myself of it,
(for the parliament committee, who logded in that
town, having notice of our coming, quitted the town
the night before, and drew most of their forces into
one head, which we broke.) From thence all that
day I continued sending to Basing House as much
wheat, malt, salt, oats, bacon, cheese, and butter, as
I could get horses and carts to transport. There I
found a little magazine of 14 barrels of powder, with
some muskets, which I likewise sent into Basing
House, and thence I sent 40 or 50 head of cattle,
with 100 sheep.

Whilst these things were doing at Basingstoke,
my lord was not wanting to himself in Basing House,
but from thence with the 100 white coats I left him,
and some of his own garrison, he sallied out into
Basing town, from whence he chased and utterly

beat the enemy, killing 40 or 50 of them, and forced the rest to retire into the park, at which place they had raised a strong fort, into which they drew all their beaten foot. In the church we took prisoners, captains Jarvise and Jephson, sons of the two most active rebels of that country, who remain prisoners in the house. At this time the day was well nigh spent, and the enemy having received some fresh supplies of horse, was more numerous and gay than in the morning, and made more show of a desire to fight with us, and advanced over a large champian, almost within musquet shot of our horse, which stood ranged in a field without Basingstoke, betwixt two hedges, lined by me with musqueteers. We stood fronting each other, till at last I perceived our squadrons of horse to grow thin, many men stealing privately out of their ranks, both our horse and men extremely tired and fasting, I ordered the horse to retire by degrees, and pass through the town towards the house, whilst I with the foot made good the avenue, or passage, on this side of the town, where the enemy appeared. And when the horse had all passed through the town, and put in their squadrons on the other side towards Basing House, I, myself, with the foot, re-tired likewise through the town, leaving captain Wills, with 60 or 70 musqueteers to secure that avenue; and being come up to our horse, I sent orders to captain Wills to retire likewise with his men, leaving only a sergeant at the avenue, with 20 musqueteers, to dispute till we were all entered into Basing House. After this I sent for the serjeant and his men, who all came off safe, the enemy not once attempting to enter into the town, but went to their quarters, not long after our horse retired. I durst not lodge that night in the town, as well because I saw the enemy multiply, and our men weary and fasting, as because of so many avenues which must have been maintained: and I feared our men would quit their guards, and betake themselves to the houses, drinking, and committing disorders in the night.

But the next day, early, I sent lieutenant colonel Buncle thither with all the horse and foot, as well to refresh the soldiers, as to be sending all that day provisions into the house.

Meanwhile I spent the day in contriving our retreat to Oxford, and sent out several spies to observe the motions of another enemy, who had formed a head from Abingdon, Newbury, and Reading, to hinder our retreat homeward.

And I found, by the unanimous relation of all my several spies, that they of Abingdon were lodged at Aldermaston, they of Newbury, at Thatcham, and they of Reading at Padworth, places adjacent

to the river Kennet, over which I was to pass in my
retreat: and that Norton, with his horse and foot,
was to follow me in the rear, whensoever I began to
march, which he conceived I could not do, but he
should have notice of it. I resolved, therefore, in
my own breast, without acquainting any man, to
make my retreat that very day, having, while there,
put at least a month's provisions into the house,
and drawn in two pieces of artillery of the enemy's,
(the one a demi-cannon) which lay betwixt the house
and the enemy's trenches, neither of them daring
adventure to draw them off. And the more to amuse
the enemy, and to cause them to think I had no in-
tention to quit so suddenly, I sent out certain war-
rants that afternoon, which I knew would fall into
his hands, to the towns of Sherbourne and Sherfield,
to bring a certain quantity of corn into the house,
upon pain, (if they refused) of sending one thousand
horse to set their towns on fire, before next day at
noon.

Having thus disposed of all things, and being
unable to serve my lord Marquis by any longer stay,
somewhat before night I sent order to lieutenant
Buncle, to retire with the men from Basingstoke,
and march to Basing House as the night before, but
not permit his men to enter the house till further
order: whither when the men were arrived, I told

my lord Marquis of my resolution to depart that
night, and of my necessity of it, and begging of him
two or three good guides, which he readily gave, I
took leave of his lordship, and began to march away,
without sound of drum or trumpet, about eleven
o'clock, that Thursday night, and gave order to all
my scouts, in case they met with any of the parliament scouts in the night, they should likewise give
themselves out to be parliament troops marching
from Basing House to the river Kennet, to lie in wait
for the Oxford forces that were to come that way.

And thus we passed the Kennet undiscovered by
a ford near Burghfield bridge (the bridge itself having been broken by the enemy) our horse taking up
the musqueteers in croup; and afterwards the Thames
by another ford at Pangbourne, within six miles of
Reading, about eight or nine o'clock upon Friday
morning. And from thence marched into the town of
Wallingford, where we rested and refreshed our
wearied men and horse that night, and the next day
arrived safe at Oxford.

Having in this expedition lost captain Sturges, a
gallant young man of the Queen's Life Guard, young
Mr. Stoner, of Oxfordshire, cornet to the troop of
Wallingford, a servant of Sir W. Hide's with some
others, to the number of eleven in all and 40 or 50
hurt, but not dangerously,

What loss the enemy had, we cannot yet learn, but we took about 100 prisoners of them. And thus, my lord, to comply with the order I received, I have troubled your lordship with a tedious relation, for which I humbly beg your pardon, and the honour to be esteemed,

My lord,

Your lordship's

Most humble servant,

HENRY GAGE.

Oxford, this 16th Sept., 1644.

Notwithstanding this gallant action and present relief of Basing, the rebels returned again, and closely besieged that place, until the 20th November following, when they gave it over before colonel Gage came, who was going a second time to raise the siege.

Oct. 4. His Majesty having now settled the affairs of the county of Dorset in the best manner either his strength or the time would possibly admit, had now good reason to have an eye, both to winter quarters, and to the relief of Banbury, Dennington, and Basing; which were still straitly besieged and reduced to very great straits, especially Banbury.

15. Certain notice that Sir William Waller was then at Andover with about 3000 horse and dragoons, it was, upon General Goring's motion, by his Ma-

jesty and the whole council, resolved, that it would exceedingly advance his Majesty's design to attempt on him there, before he was joined with Essex's forces, (who, at this time, were about Basing) and if that succeeded we might with more ease endeavour the relief of Basing, Dennington, &c.

18. As it was, they were scattered and made haste away, being closely pursued by our horse until the darkness of the night hindered any more action, and gave them the opportunity in this terror to fly through Whitchurch to Basing and Newbury.

His Majesty and his army quartered that night at Andover, and concluding the next morning that this beating up of Waller, dispersing his forces, would put a terror into the rest, he resolved to march forward; and to that end sent order, that all his soldiers, cannon, and baggage, left at Salisbury and Wilton, should instantly follow him, as likewise the Earl of Cleveland, and the foot that were now on their march after the relief of Portland.

Whereupon his Majesty and that part of his army marched to Whitchurch, where he staid until Monday, the 21st, by which time all his force was come up. This speedy advance at that time was by some esteemed the first and only error that had been committed since his Majesty left Oxford, for now we were engaged and could not in honour retreat, neither could we give any relief to Basing, the rebels then lying about it.

Oct. 21. On Monday, the 21st of October, his Majesty, with his whole army, marched from Whitchurch to Kingsclere, which is an equal distance between Basing and Newbury, with intentions to have stayed there the next day, and thence to have attempted the relief of Basing; but that being too open a place, and the rebels stronger in horse, we marched from thence on Tuesday to Newbury.

Part of the king's army were sent to relieve Banbury, which they effected on the very day of the month that both town and castle were rendered to his Majesty two years since, being the 26th of Oct.

His Majesty, in the interim, lay still at Newbury, where he seriously considered the speediest ways to relieve Basing; and then cause his army so to be quartered as to do but little duty, and yet to be secure from the rebels, who (it was thought) would not attempt us in that place, and whence his Majesty could not remove, conveniently, until he had done his endeavours for the relief of Basing; and that the Earl of Northampton, with that addition of strength he took with him to Banbury was returned.

The rebels being reinforced with foot and horse, and in obedience to the order of their masters at Westminster which were positive to fight with his

Majesty, he drew from Basing on Tuesday, the 22nd, and lay the two next days in Aldermaston park.

Nov. 8.   Here you must know that his Majesty made the greater haste, first to disengage his ordnance in Dennington, and to put some relief into that place; and above all to the relief of Basing, still besieged by the rebels.

A few days previous to this date, the king conferred the honour of knighthood on colonel Gage, who, in his Majesty's absence, had so well deserved, both in the defence of Oxford, and the relief of Banbury and Basing.

Nov. 12.   On Tuesday, the 12th of November, his Majesty and the army came to Marlborough, where he found good effects of the endeavours of the lords Capell, Hopton, Culpepper; and the treasurer at war, and much provision prepared, and more designed, as well for the support of the army, as to be sent into Dennington, (not sufficiently stored) and to be carried with the army, or with a party, for the relief of Basing: for this was now the question, whether we should attempt the relief of that place with the whole or a party: at length it was concluded that the safest course would be to do it by a party.   And Sir Henry Gage (who had once before with so good success relieved that garrison) was made choice of, who was to endeavour it in this manner;

to have with him 1000 horse, every one of which was to carry before him a bag of corn, or other provisions, and he to march so as to be at Basing House the next morning after he parted from the army; and there every trooper to cast down his bag, and then to make his retreat good as well they might. This design colonel Gage cheerfully undertook; and the better to effect it, Hungerford was thought a fitter place to quarter with the army, and thence to despatch him on this enterprise: whither on Sunday, the 17th of Nov., his Majesty and the army marched. In the interim, the rebels removed from Newbury to Aldermaston, and so about Basing, where, apprehending it not possible to gain that place, and being weary of this winter war, they quitted the siege the day before Sir Henry Gage came thither, and retired all into their winter quarters.

Nov. 21. On the 21st, his Majesty marched to Faringdon, and stayed there a day to expect the issue of the design for Basing, and to consider where to make his winter quarters, in which time his Majesty had certain intelligence that the rebels were gone thence, that Sir Henry Gage had put in the provisions and was upon his march back, which good success was above our expectation.

After the battle of Alresford, Sir W. Waller's first and principal design was to surprise Basing House, by a correspondence with the lord Edward Pawlet, brother to the marquis of Winchester, and then, with him, as unsuspected as a brother ought to be. For the better execution of this, Sir R. Grenvil was sent before with a body of the horse, that all things might be well disposed, and prepared against the time Waller himself should come to him. He appointed a rendezvous for the horse at Bagshot, and the same day marched out of London only with his equipage; which was very noble; a coach and six horses; a waggon and six horses; many led horses, and many servants: with those, when he came to Staines, he left the Bagshot road and marched directly to Reading, where the king's garrison then was; and thence, without delay, to Oxford; where he was very graciously received by the king, and the more because he was not expected. He communicated then to the king the whole design of the surprise of Basing; upon which the king sent express immediately to the Marquis, with all the particular informations; who thereupon seized upon his brother, and the other conspirators; who confessed all, with all the circumstances of the correspondence and combination. The marquis prevailed with the king that he might only turn his brother out of the garrison, after justice had been done upon his accomplices. This very happy and seasonable discovery, preserved that important place; which, without it, had infallibly been lost within a few days, and therefore could not but much endear the person of the discoverer; upon whom the parliament thundered out all those reproaches which his deserting them in such a manner was liable to : and denounced all those judgments on him of attainder, confiscation, and incapacity of pardon, which they used to do against those, who they thought, had done them most mischief, or against whom they were most incensed : which was all the excuse he could make for his severe proceedings against those of their party who fell into his hands afterward where he commanded. *

The final investment of Basing House appears to have been undertaken by Cromwell. When the king's cause declined every where, this general came with his victorious troops out of the west, and attacked Basing House, and so vigorously pushed on the siege, that the royalists saw it was impossible for them to hold out as they had formerly done, and therefore desired a parley; but Oliver was resolved to chastise them for their obstinate loyalty, and would hearken to no proposals, intending to take it

* Clarendon's History of the Rebellion, &c., Vol. II. p. 414.

by storm. Having, therefore, posted his army round the house, the attack was begun, and Sir Hardress Waller's and Col. Montague's regiments, having forced the works of the besieged, mounted the walls and entered the house before the defendants perceived their danger. There is a traditionary report, that the garrison was partly surprised, through some of the troops being engaged at cards when the assault commenced. *   Basing House, which held out so long, and had been thought almost impregnable, was at length taken by storm, October the 14th, 1645, and burnt to the ground, in despite of the *Aimez Loyaulté*, which the valiant Marquis had written in every window.† Seventy-two men were lost on the king's side, and about 200 (another account says 400) taken prisoners, among whom was the Marquis himself, and several other persons of distinction, whom Cromwell sent up to the parliament, and received the thanks of the house for these successful services.

Among the distinguished persons taken prisoners, was Sir Robert Peake, who commanded the garrison under the Marquis. Lieutenant colonel Wiborn, and

---

* It is said, card players of the neighbourhood have a common saying of " Clubs Trumps, as when Basing House was taken."

† Beauties of England and Wales.

serjeant major Cufaude, of the royalists, are said to
have been slain in cold blood.*   Dr. Thos. Johnson,
the celebrated botanist, being with the royal army,
received a wound of which he died.   Six [catholic]
priests were also among the slain.†   Robinson, a
stage player, was killed by Major General Har-
rison, who is said to have refused him quarter,
and shot him in the head, when he had laid
down his arms, with this quotation from scripture;
"Cursed is he that doeth the work of the Lord
negligently,"‡   Hollar, the celebrated engraver,
who was there at the time, made his escape. Dr.
Thomas Fuller, author of the Church History of
Britain, and other works, being chaplain in the royal
army, under lord Hopton, was for some time shut
up in Basing House, while it was besieged.   Even
here, as if sitting in the study of a quiet parsonage,
far removed from the din of war, he prosecuted his
favourite work, entitled, 'The Worthies of England,'
discovering no sign of fear, but only complaining
that the noise of the cannon, which was continually
thundering from the lines of the besiegers inter-

* Sir J. Prestwick's Republica.

† Vicar's Parliamentary Chronicle.

‡ Davies's Life of Garrick.

rupted him in digesting his notes.* Dr. Fuller, however, animated the garrison to so vigorous a defence, that Sir William Waller was obliged to raise the siege with considerable loss, by which the fate of Basing House was, for a considerable time suspended. When it was besieged a second time, and fell, lord Hopton's army took shelter in the city of Exeter, whither Fuller accompanied it.†

Captain Wilks, in the parliament army, was slain, Sir Gilbert Pickering, in the same service, distinguished himself, especially with his brigade, in the storming of Basing House, where he commanded in chief, as he had done in the storming of Bristol, and Lacock House.‡ The number of men slain before the walls, from the first commencement of the siege, is recorded to have exceeded 2000. The plunder obtained, on this occasion, is said to have amounted to £200,000, in cash, jewels, and furniture, among which was a bed worth £1400.§ A private soldier is said to have received £300, as his

---

* This indifference of the facetious Fuller, in time of danger, reminds us of a water carrier, who, during the time of a siege, was going about crying, " water, three-pence a bucket." A bomb shell took away one of his buckets, " Six-pence a bucket," he then cried, and went on.

† Christian Observer, Aug. 1805.   ‡ Noble's Life of Cromwell.

§ Other accounts say, £14,000. Horace Walpole with great propriety asks, of what was composed the bed, valued at £14,000·

share of the booty. Babbling fame has reported that Mrs. Cromwell coveted a part of the spoils of war, and that she amassed great quantities of jewels, medals, &c., from the plunder of various houses; Basing in particular, where the soldiery, by command, or for small gratuities, were persuaded to give up several portions of the spoil. The lady-receiver was seen to be very pleasant at the enjoyment of those pretty things, as she called them, being the best for substance and ornament, that belonged to the noble Marquis and his family, which she now catalogued for her own.*

An aged person, who died lately at Basingstoke, had in his possession a Bible, which he said his grandfather found on a table in Basing House having attended Cromwell at the time it was taken. As the Marquis was a catholic, this Bible, being of the Geneva edition, (which the compiler of these pages has seen) probably belonged to some protestant engaged in the royal cause.

Hugh Peters was at the taking of Basing House, and being come to London, to make a report if it to the parliament, said, it was a house fit for an emperor to live in, it was so spacious and beautiful. The Marchioness of Winchester, second wife of the

---

* Court and Character of the Protectress.

Marquis, was distinguished for courage and prudence, like the celebrated Blanche, lady Arundel, who so nobly defended Wardour Castle. The Marchioness valiantly aided in the defence of Basing House, which was taken during her absence. She wrote a Journal of the proceedings relative to the siege.

In time of warfare, and particularly during a long protracted siege, the surrounding neighbourhood has always suffered distressing injuries from the soldiery. It is recorded, that it is incredible what booty the garrison of this place picked up, lying, as they did, just on the great western road, where they intercepted the carriers, plundered the waggons, and suffered nothing to pass, to the great interruption of the trade of the city of London. The gaining of Basing House, though calamitous to the royal cause, and the noble owner, was reckoned a great piece of service to the nation, whereby the road was open for trade from London to the west, which had been so long obstructed.

It was probably on this occasion, that the " Sign of Basing House" became exhibited as the attractive sign of an Inn, near Shore Ditch, in London, and which exist to the present day.*

It is said that the Holy Ghost Chapel, at Basingstoke, was then stripped of its covering of lead to

---

* Gentlemen's Mag., 1806, p. 1169.

make balls for the use of the besiegers of Basing
House. In the same neighbourhood, Farleigh House
was made a garrison for the parliament, when the in-
scriptions, and all the brass plate in the church,
were taken away.*   There is a field situated on the
right of the road leading from Basingstoke, near the
bridge over the canal, which is called *Slaughter
Close*. It is traditionally said to have been the scene
of sanguinary contests, at a time when the garrison
made a sally to obstruct, or destroy, the offensive
works of the besiegers. The slain on both sides were
buried in this field, which, it is said to this day,
produces the most abundant crops of every thing
sown in it. The reader may be shocked at the idea
of an harvest being produced by the rich manure of
human carcases; but philosophy, as well as poetry,
teaches us, that the affecting truth exists, not only
at Basing, but elsewhere also.

> Where is the dust that has not been alive?
> The spade, the plough, disturb our ancestors;
> From human mould we reap our daily bread.
> As nature wide, our ruins spread; man's death
> Inhabits all things, but the thought of man.

The late Mr. Moses Barton Legg, of Basingstoke,
(afterwards of Basing) was a person rather curious
in his enquiries respecting the antiquities of the

---

* Warner's Collections.

neighbourhood. From a paper of memoranda, in his hand writing, containing some particulars of Basing, we present to the reader the following extracts.

Aug. 29, 1798.

"Walked with James Exall up Back Lane, which he supposes was formerly a street, where he pointed out some old brick-work, to all appearance the remains of the foundation of a house. We went to the ruins of Basing house, where he pointed out the spot where the original house stood, and the cellars, on the east of the gate-way; two arches of brick-work crossing and directly over each other; several pieces of wood, cinder, and burnt tile, which seem to show that the buildings were set on fire after the house was taken. The oblong flat in front of the keep was a bowling green, and kept in order since his recollection. There were several large fir trees on it, which were cut down by Charles, Duke of Bolton. Round the top of the keep, was a parapet wall, full four feet high above the gravel walk; part of the gravel now remains.

"After the original house was destroyed, a mansion was build on the north side of the road opposite the ruins. The piers, of fine jointed brick-work, were the entrance to the mansion, which was pulled down 50 or 60 years ago by the then Duke, and the materials carried to Kingsclere.*

"In a field near the brick bridge, called Slaughter Close, an old oak pollard, containing 7 or 8 cord of wood, was cut down about 20 years ago, and given for fire wood. Exall saw it split up, and a great number of musket balls taken out of it.

"*Pitch Croft*, a piece of ground, the more proper name of which is *Priest Croft*, appears to have been a fort. There was a house, &c., there formerly, said to have been the residence of a priest, officiated at Basing House.

"Most of the foregoing particulars he had from one Moss, an old man of 93 years, or upwards, who died about 30 years ago.

"1800, March 1st. Went to look at the ruins, and met lord Bolton, when I had a long conversation with his lordship. He pointed out the alterations he intended to make, as he took great delight in the place. On expressing my regret that there was no drawing of the original house, &c., extant, at least that I could hear of, he told me that he had one; pointed out the spot where the original house stood, which was exactly the same as Exall told me on the 29th of Aug. last; also, that the one which stood on the north side of the road was a subsequent erection; for after

* With part of the materials was built the George Inn, at Basingstoke.

the original mansion was taken by Oliver's forces, it was set fire to and destroyed, with most of the valuable paintings, papers, &c."

In digging the canal at Basing, several human skeletons, cannon balls, coins, and other ancient articles, were found, some of which have been preserved by different persons. An immense old chalk pit, a little to the north of Basing, is still known by the name of *Oliver Cromwell's Dell*, where, perhaps, his troops might sometimes retire during the siege.

It appears, from a survey made in the year 1798, that the area of the works, including the garden and entrenchments, occupied about fourteen acres and a half. The form was extremely irregular; the ditches very deep, and the ramparts high and strong : some of the remains are yet very bold and striking. The citadel was circular, having an oblong square platform at the north, defended by a rampart and covered way. The north gate-way is yet standing ; which, surmounted with venerable ivy, concealing the ancient arms of the PAWLETTS, constitutes a fine relic of the former grandeur of the place, and is certainly worthy of being kept in a state of preservation. Parts of the outward walls, constructed with brick, still remain. The site of the ruins is particularly commanding ; the canal from Basingstoke has been cut through part of the works, and

the outward entrenchments have been rendered very
obscure and imperfect from some late improvements
in the ground. The medium depth of the fosse,
which surrounded the citadel, is about thirty-six
feet perpendicular.

The brave Marquis, whose property was thus reduced to ruin, in the cause of his sovereign, lived till
the restoration, but received no recompense from an
ungrateful court for his immense losses. His loyalty
was the more remarkable, as coming from a catholic
subject to a protestant king. During the latter part
of his life, he resided at Englefield, in Berkshire,
where he built a noble mansion, the front of which
resembled a church organ, but it has suffered by
some late modernizations. Dying in 1674, he was
buried there in the parish church; the epitaph on
his monument was written by the poet Dryden, and
is as follows:—

> He who in impious times undaunted stood,
> And 'midst rebellion durst be just and good;
> Whose arms asserted, and whose sufferings more
> Confirmed the cause for which he fought before;
> Rests here; rewarded by an heavenly prince,
> For what his earthly could not recompense.
> Pray, reader, that such times no more appear;
> Or, if they happen, learn true honour here.
> Ark of this age's faith and loyalty,
> Which to preserve them heaven confin'd in thee.
> Few subjects could a king like thine deserve,
> And fewer such a king so well could serve.
> Blest king, blest subject, whose exalted state
> By suffering rose, and gave the law to fate.
> Such souls are rare, but mighty patterns giv'n
> To earth, and meant for ornaments to heaven.

The Marquis translated from the French, the "Gallery of Heroic Women; 1653, and Talon's "Holy History;" 1652. See a copy of verses on the Marquis of Winchester's Gallery of Ladies," in Howell's Letter, vol. IV.

The first wife of the Marquis was Jane, the very accomplished daughter of Thomas, Viscount Savage; she was taught Spanish by James Howell, Esq., who addressed a very curious letter to her grace. See his "Familiar Letters," vol. I. She was the mother of Charles, first Duke of Bolton, but died in the delivery of her second child, in the 24th year of her age. An epitaph to her memory was written by Milton. There was also a Cambridge collection of verses on her death, among which Milton's lines appeared being written while he was a student at Christ's College.* It is well known that the author of 'Paradise Lost,' became latin secretary to Cromwell. Ben Johnson wrote an elegy on the Lady Ann Pawlett, Marchioness of Winchester; she was a lady of great honour and alliance, as sister to the Earl of Essex, and to the lady Marchiones of Hertford.†

Among the numerous portraits at Hackwood Park, is a full length of John Pawlett,‡ fifth Marquis; also a full length of the Marchioness, his second wife. A small oval portrait of this nobleman has been en-

---

* Topographer.   † Clarendon.

‡ This noble family have spelt their names differently, viz., POWLET, PAWLET, and PAULET.

graved by Hollar, who engraved also a small view of Basing House, which is extremely rare.

It is remarkable that another John Pawlet, advanced by Charles I. to the dignity of a baron of the realm, by the title of Lord Pawlet, of Hinton St. George, in Somersetshire, (descended from the original family of the Pawlets, of Pawlet, in that county, whence the surname was taken) manifested his loyalty also to the king, in the civil wars. In 1644, he was one of the principal commanders that besieged Lyme, in Dorsetshire; and the same year met his majesty a mile from Exeter, in order to conduct him to that city; and afterwards had the honour to entertain him at his seat at Hinton St. George. He was a considerable sufferer in the royal cause, as was also his son, Sir John Pawlet, who was engaged with him on the same side.

The following lines, from a latin epitaph, on a noble monument erected to one of their ancestors, in the church of St Martin's in the Fields, London, may, with the alteration of one word, be applied to the noble defender of Basing House, in allusion to the famous *Aimez Loyaulté,* and the three swords in the family arms :—

> Quod verbo servare, PAULETE, solebas;
> Quam bene conveniunt næc *duo* verba tibi.
> Quod gladio servare fidem, PAULETE, solebas,
> Quam bene conveniunt hæc tria signa tibi.*

* Topographer, vol. I.

It is said that our great moralist, Dr. Johnson, on being asked why he did not oftener read history, answered, "I do not love to read the annals of blood." It is, doubtless, painful to the feelings of humanity to peruse the histories of war, especially the civil wars of our own country, and the destructive sieges by which strong castles and princely mansions have been won and lost. But the perusal may be useful, as we naturally wish to know what has been transacted in centuries that are past, and especially in our own neighbourhood. When we visit the affecting ruins, and discover the desolation which war has occasioned, we wish to know something of the history of the men, who have performed such mighty, but destructive deeds. It may be useful to compare the present internal condition of our native country, with that which it has presented within the short space of 700 years. At the commencement of the reign of Henry II., in 1133, there were more than a thousand fortified castles in the country. Those days exhibited little less than intestine broils, discord, and rapine of the feudal system. If Basing and Odiham castles in our own neighbourhood, and many others in the kingdom, no longer exhibit their warlike towers, and stately walls, in the posture of defence, we are thankful they are no longer needful. Let us contemplate the delightful change which the internal state of England presents in our own times. Now we behold

in the aspect of nobility, a philanthrophy and be-
nignity diffusing real blessings, in the patronage of
every institution, which has for its object, the in-
struction of the ignorant, the relief of suffering humanity, and the general amelioration of society.
Education, like a mighty torrent, is spreading its
enlightening influence into every hamlet of our
country, dispelling, in its progress, the debasing
prejudice, and slavish superstition, of years haply
gone by: and we discover in the intelligence of our
population, the surest criterion of eternal peace.
The benign influence of Christianity has produced
the pleasing change. The present little history may,
perhaps, excite in the breast of the reader the happy
sensation of gratitude, that it is the history of times
and events long since past, as we hope, to return
no more.

APPENDIX.

Containing full Particulars of the Assault and Capture of Basing House.

———

A granado from us killed the countess of Winchester's waiting maid; and it seems before the house was begirt round. A party of their's surprised col Hammond, a commander of ours, the enemy stealing out on a foggy night, but although it was his hap to be taken, yet we have good assurance that the house will be taken by lieut. gen. Cromwell and col. Dalbier, within a few days, for besides the battery formerly made, lieut. gen. Cromwell is raising forts and sconces about the house, which, within a few days will be brought to good perfection. The two commanders, col. Hammond and major King, were going out of Basing town to view the horse that were on the other side of the house, and it being a great fog, a party of the enemy were stolen a little way out of the house, and met with col. Hammond and major King, who knew them not, nor scarce saw them, till they were within pistol shot. They were both taken and carried into the house; whereupon lieut. col. Cromwell wrote a letter, acquainting the governor, that if any wrong or violence were offered those men, the best in the house should not obtain quarter. About twelve of the clock this day, (the 8th of October,) came two messengers, one after the other, with intelligence to the house, that Basing was taken about 6 or 7 o'clock this morning by storm. The messengers were both called into the house, and the relation of the whole besiegers communicated.

L. G. C. having planted his ordnance against the south-east part of the house, and made all things in readiness, began his battery an Friday last; col. Dalbier continuing his battery where he had first began, on that side of the new house next the church. Our cannoneers shewed excellent skill, and lost few shot; in the interim, our horse and foot stood entire, only some few (without command) rode down near the very walls, and gave fire at the enemy. By Monday night our ordnance had done such execution, both on the part of the house, where col. Dalbier placed his battery, and likewise where L. G. C. had placed his, that our men might enter; and the next morning (that is to say this present Tuesday), at day-break we began the storm; and our soldiers, with undaunted courage, got over the enemy's works, entered the breaches, and possessed part of the new house, and the court, betwixt that and the old house, where the enemy had lain a train of powder, which they blew up, the quantity was thought to be about three barrels, but, blessed be God, it did not much annoy us. This being done, our men slid in at the windows, and compassed the new house round, for the enemy were fled thither, then they in the house threw hand granadoes out of the house, at our men, into the court; but we made our passage into the house amongst them, and, by force of arms, appeased their rage, and at the coming away of the messengers the storm was ended, and our men possessed of all, both new and old houses. The whole storm, from the beginning to the end, was not above three quarters of an hour. The certainty of what loss was on both sides is not yet known, but it is affirmed, we lost but one man e'er we got within their works. The day before we stormed it, they turned all their prisoners out of the house, save only col. Hammond, and major King, who are preserved and well. In the house was the marquis of Winchester, (but his lady got away on Wednesday) and a great many commanders and persons of quality, and of common soldiers, by estimation, about 600, most whereof papists, and fought desperately, and are all either killed or taken. There was also about 7 pieces of ordnance, great store of ammunition, and rich treasure.

Col. Hammond, who was taken prisoner, came this day unto the House of Commons, and made a more full relation of the taking of Basing House, in the manner as was before expressed. The Marquis and Sir Robert Peake were preserved by the captivity of col Hammond. Sir Robert Peake gave col. Hammond the key of his chamber, but the plunder was taken by the soldiers, before he could find his way into it; Robinson, the player, was taken there, he was in Drury Lane, a comedian, but now he acted his own tragedy; there were taken also the marquis, his major, 400 quarters of wheat, and 300 flitches of bacon; the number of slain and taken are yet doubtful; some say we have lost but forty men, some say we have killed 300 of the enemy, some say more. But this as yet (for we have no perfect list brought yet) is very uncertain. *Diary, or an ex. Journal Oct. 9 to 16.*

A further relation was this day brought to the House by col. Hammond, of the taking of Basing, as also lieutenant general Cromwell's own letter thereof to the speaker of the House of Commons, which, for better satisfaction, follows:

Sir,

"I thank God, I can give some account of Basing. After our batteries were placed, we settled the several posts for the storme; col. Dalbier was to be on the north side of the house next the Grange; col. Pickering on his left hand, and Sir Hardresse Waller's and col. Montague's regiment next him. We stormed this morning after six of the clocke; the signal for falling on was the firing 4 of our cannon, which, being done, our men fell on with great resolution and cheerfulness; we took the two houses without any considerable losse to ourselves. Col. Pickering stormed the new house, passed through, and got the gate of the old house, whereupon they summoned a parley which our men would not heare. In the mean time, col. Montague's and Sir Hardresse Waller's regiments assaulted the strongest work, where the enemy kept his court of guard, which, with great resolution, they recovered; beating the enemy from a whole culverin, and from that work; which having done, they drew their ladders after them, and got over another work, and the house wall, before they could enter. In this, Sir Hardresse Waller, performed his duty with honour and diligence, was shot on the arm, but not dangerous; we have had little loss; many of the enemy our men put to the sword, and some officers of quality, most of the rest we have prisoners, among which, the marquis and Sir Robert Peake, with divers other officers, whom I have ordered to be sent up to you. We have taken about ten pieces of ordnance, with much ammunition, and our soldiers a good encouragement. I humbly offer to you, to have this place entirely slighted, for three following reasons :—

It will take 800 men to manage it; it is no frontier; the country is poor about it; the place exceedingly ruined by our batteries, and mortar pieces, and a fire which fell upon the place since our taking it. If you please to take the garrison at Farnham, some out of Chichester, and a good part of the foot which were under Dalbier, and make a strong quarter at

Newbury with three or four troop of horse; I dare
be confident it would not only be a curb to Dennington, but a security and frontier to all these parts, in
as much as Newbury lies on the river, and will pre-
vent any incursion from Dennington, Wallingford, or
Farrington, into these parts, and by lying there will
make the trade most secure for all carriages. And
I believe the gentlemen of Sussex and Hampshire,
will, with more cheerfulness, contribute to maintain
a garrison on the frontier than in their bowells, which
will have less safety in it; sir, I hope not to delay,
but march towards the west to-morrow; and be as
diligent as I may, in my expedition thither; I must
speak my judgment to you, that if you intend to have
your work carried on, recruits of foot must be had,
and a course taken to pay your army, else believe me,
sir, it may not be able to answer the work, you have
for it to do. I entrusted col. Hammond to wait upon
you, who was taken by a mistake while we lay before
this garrison, whom God safely delivered to us, to
our great joy; but to his loss of almost all he had,
which the enemy took from him. The Lord grant
that these mercies may be acknowledged with all
thankfulness; God exceedingly abounds in his good-
ness to us, and will not be weary until righteousness
and peace meet, and that he hath brought forth a
glorious work for the happiness of this poor kingdom,

wherein desires to serve God and you with a faithful
hand, Your most hum. Ser.

OLIVER CROMWELL."

Basingstoke,
14 Oct. 1645.

———

The most perfect list of the prisoners and prizes
taken according to the relation of colonel Hammond,
master Peters,* and others, is as followeth : prisoners
taken, the Marquis of Winchester, Sir Robt. Peake,
Dr. Griffith, and 4 popish priests; about 200 other
prisoners, whereof some of note ; slain, major Robinson, major Cuffles, and in view about 74 others, and
only one woman, the daughter of Dr. Griffith; ten
pieces of ordnance, twenty barrels of powder, and
matches proportionable, nine colours, two hundred
arms, two hundred horse, the rooms and chambers in
both houses completely furnished, which afforded the
soldiers gallant pillage; provisions of victuals for
some years rather than months, 400 quarters of
wheat, 300 flitches of bacon, 200 barrels of beef,
40,000lbs. of cheese, beer, divers cellars full, and
that very good. A bed in one room, furnished, cost
£1,300, great store of popish books, with copes,
and such utensils: silver plate, valued at £5000,
some cabinets of jewels, and other treasure; one
soldier had six score pieces of gold for his share,

---

* Hugh Peters was executed at the Restoration, because he had contributed
by his Sermons, perhaps to the death of Charles I. MONTHLY MAG.

and another had got three bags of silver, who, (not able to keep his own counsel,) it grew to common pillage among the rest, the fellow at last having but one half-a-crown for himself. The wheat, household goods, and lumber, with a great part of the other pillage, was sold to the country people, who likewise had a good part of the prey, and carried many cart loads away, the house was burnt down and demolished. A letter this. day come from lieut. general Cromwell, from Wallop, of the 16th of October present, which was read in the House, of his intentions and designs of that armies' march westward, to join Sir Thomas Fairfax. And the house thereupon ordered, that the advance and motion of Sir Thomas Fairfax's army, and that part thereof under the command of lieutenant general Cromwell, should be left to themselves, for the best advantage of the kingdom, having regard for the safety of the west; and it was also ordered, that lieutenant general Cromwell should continue his command of lieutenant general Cromwell to Sir Thomas Fairfax, after the expiration of his former time, for four months longer.

The interesting documents which follow, were kindly furnished by C. E. Lefroy, Esq., West Ham.

The 3rd of July, 1644, a musket ball passed through the clothes of the marquis, and on the 22nd he was wounded by another. A journal of the siege, printed at Oxford, minutely records every day's work. It preserves also two short letters from the marquis. On the 11th of July, colonel Morly, then commanding the besiegers, (in the absence of colonel Norton), having in stern, but civil terms, summoned the garrison to surrender, the marquis replied,

SIR,

It is a crooked demand, and shall receive its answer suitable. I keep the house in the right of my sovereign, and will do it in despite of your forces; your letter I will preserve in testimony of your rebellion.

WINCHESTER.

To another summons, from Norton himself on the 2nd of September, the marquis replied,

SIR,

Whereas you demand the House and garrison of Basing by a pretended authority of parliament, I make this answer: that without the king there can be no parliament: by his Majesty's commission I keep this place, and without his absolute command, shall not deliver it to any pretenders whatever.

Your's, to serve you,

WINCHESTER.

Chandler, Printer, Basingstoke.